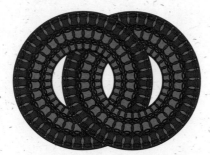

The Bar of the Flattened Heart

DAVID KELLER

The Bar of the Flattened Heart

POEMS

CavanKerry ◈ Press LTD.

CavanKerry Press Ltd.
Fort Lee, New Jersey
www.cavankerrypress.org

Publisher's Cataloging-in-Publication
(Provided by Quality Books, Inc.)

Keller, David, 1941–
The bar of the flattened heart : poems / David Keller.
pages cm
Poems.
ISBN 978-1-933880-42-6

I. Title.

PS3561.E3852B37 2014   811'.54
QBI14-600062

Cover photo by Lynn Betts, USDA Natural Resources Conservation Service
Cover and interior design by Gregory Smith
First Edition 2014, Printed in the United States of America

CavanKerry Press is proud to publish the works
of established poets of merit and distinction.

CavanKerry Press is grateful for the support it receives
from the New Jersey State Council on the Arts.

OTHER BOOKS BY DAVID KELLER

Circling the Site

A New Room

Land That Wasn't Ours

Trouble in History

to the memory of Donald Sheehan and Jack Wiler

While you been stepping out, someone else

been stepping in.

—Denise LaSalle

Contents

I

II

The Bar of the Flattened Heart

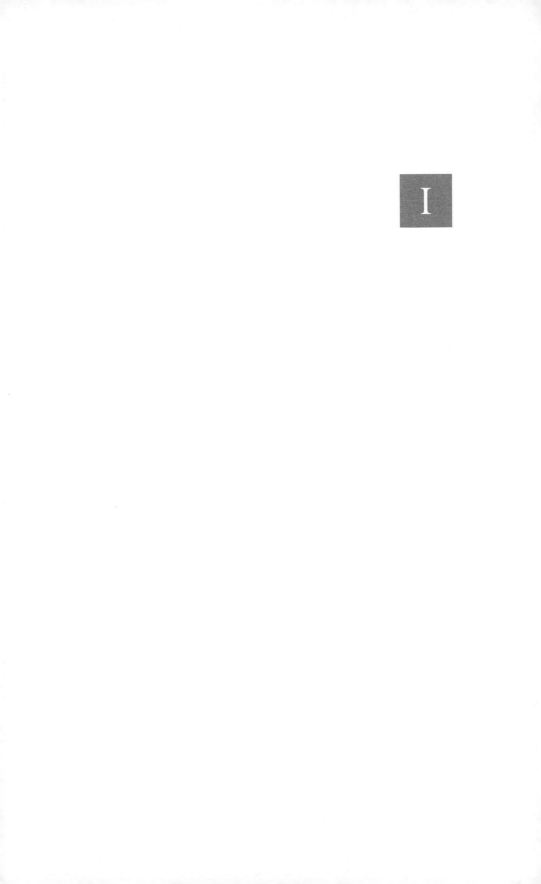

I

Last Night As the Dog

                                        shoved his way
out from under the covers at the bottom
of the bed and padded off, I thought
how foresighted of us to have comforters
rather than blankets
holding down the bottom of the sheets.
Otherwise he'd have to wake us, or the cold would,
every time he got up for the sofa, or his own bed.

And I thought of my ex-wife, and how cold
the bedroom was kept at night
to save money. We'd pile on blankets,
layer after layer, and though warm,
it was almost suffocating,
like the dead under the heavy weight
of grass and dirt after darkness seeps
up from the trees and lawns into the air.

That's what I've made up,
to remember at odd moments. And, of course,
my enduring, heroic self. Perhaps
he did not want to be trapped beneath the covers,
where it's like the caves
I made as a child. I'm always amazed
by how long he lasts
before he wants to be in the chill air.

On walks in the morning,
the dog will nose his way, place to place,
as if the dead might be there, or there
just beyond us, while I trail behind.

At night he will scramble back into the bed,
into the cave beyond memory,
to have my wife hold up the covers, half-asleep,
so he can lie down the way memory does,
or the soft dark I live in, less easily.

Afternoon on Cake Street

It was late in January, she said it was
almost 20 below when the boy came in
from delivering his newspapers. It was late, oh
late, and she'd worried he was in trouble.

He'd dropped his newspapers at each house
along the country route, like stones or
breadcrumbs, and he'd kept warm
in the lobbies of the two apartment buildings;

so he had not noticed the cold
clutching at the streets and telephone poles
in the grey of late afternoon, the dark
coming on amidst swirls of snow and ice.

He had walked in the kitchen door alive
for dinner as usual and said nothing. Yet
after that winter each gorgeous fall became,
without his knowing how he knew, a test

that would grow more severe each year.
Yet he did not die in the woods and small streets
along his way. Each year he would forget
the brilliant colors of the leaves falling

as they are today, the yellow sunlight
of sweet-gum leaves, far from his youth,
as if each autumn were something to recall
after passing on to somewhere new.

Until this time he had never known the agonies parents
feel over raising children in danger.
He knew she had wanted him dead back then,
though it had taken him a lifetime to be certain,

and that the days from this fall would vanish, too,
along with what the child had felt for his mother
and the world in all its colors and breath he had admired
but never trusted. He felt warm and beloved.

An Anniversarie

And isn't the past inevitable,
now that we call the little
we remember of it "the past"?

    —William Matthews

I was listening to the DVD
of *Beyond the Fringe*, which I saw
—was it '63?—and in a side interview
with Alan Bennett, he was asked if,
like other people, he had regrets
about his life. Yes, of course. And they were?
I can't remember, he replied.

He would say that. Bits of fondness
are what I'd say, along with the rest,
now that it's been ten years since we split up,
so here's an anniversary of sorts, ten years,
a mere twinkling, though half a lifetime
for the kids I taught just last year.
What do they know about time?

Sic transit gloria mundi? No,
not her. Ruby Tuesday? Never.
Hoping you are well, I remain, fondly,

Your ex-husband

The Way of My Education

Hat in the air's one way to say it,
or, thinking like dancing.
The man with the hat in the Magritte
has no head. It floats above him,
above what he knows of the world.
Here inside the window
flowers shift and shimmer like sounds.

How long is a year
or a 45-foot anaconda? One could measure
but not know. Or is it
to understand without measuring?
The second time you see the painting,
it's still amusing, but like a concept. There. Now
who wants a story? Thank you.

Every time my parents asked me
to do something with my mind,
I responded with my hands.
I'm sorry the world shrinks.
I can walk upon the surface
of a piece of paper, leaving
sparks that look like stars
and more stars.

It is not "monkey business" when you think
of the experiment where the two men
measured the speed of light
using a surface the size of a ping-pong table.

May pearls come before spring swine,
er, I mean the sunshine. Oh let's all go down
to the Homer Spit
and spit in the cold, geometric water.

As the Twelfth Armored Division Enters the Capital

for Renee

1

I am taking my dick for a walk tonight
though we must not say so. I have a reputation
to maintain, the shameless postures
I have had to cover up, not to mention a wife
and what I said to women who knew me
under cover of darkness or before dawn

when we went out. Like the news, I take it for granted;
it is hardly mine, any more than
the sidewalk is. But here we are,
out for a walk or a peaceful cigarette
in the old Iraqi city, its ancient palaces
still a reminder of some other decency
though there is neither bud nor blossom left.

2

There is nothing I can say to
the cruel man who orders someone
to give him a blow job, never mind who. He will not make
a single sound, though his whole body
cries out for it, for music, so as not to give
anything of himself away.

We have settled into a truce of sorts, me and my dick.
I no longer accuse it of lacking passion,
the desire to conquer everything, and, for its part,
there are whole nights of sleep given me
without its restless arithmetic, the dull
biographies longing for a publisher.

3

Gone are the petty jokes, the exaggerations, even
though we are not passing places it is dangerous to be seen in.
And what was there in the line
the other jerkoffs I spent my teenage
years with repeated almost nightly,
saying to someone, "It's so nice out
tonight, I think I'll leave it out all night"?

The Octopus

The warm shadows are back along the streets,
and the world loves us again, so lovely,
like the small octopus in a tank,
an exhibit for children. See it there,
its tentacles like gauze stretching
along the sides of the tank. If I tap,
one tentacle or another reaches upward
toward my finger, a ghostlike and translucent
blue-grey. How impossibly delicate
it seems, each sucker independently
holding or releasing, the limb
like the large fire engines in Boston
with the second man driving the back wheels
around the city streets, and the other,

so that each tentacle seems under
its own control, slowly waving along the tank

toward my fingers on the glass.
There is a sign off to one side,
informing us that the octopus "sees"
by feeling pressure waves, which I imagine
is what my tapping brings up,
though my fanciful wife suggests
that the tentacles long for some connection
to me. Touching, one might say.
Tasting is more likely the case.
The water, too, seems as warm and forgiving
as the air in the small exhibit room
where children come to learn about touch,
about the gauzy longing like hunger in them.
It is spring, and in us too.

Classified

I have radioactive dinner plates. Not because they were exposed
to radiation in Los Alamos, where my father worked, where I
remember guards by what seems a fountain, oh, highly unlikely
on the top of that New Mexico mesa, and around a barbed-wire
enclosure, carrying Tommy guns as I waved my father Happy
New Work and Goodbye.

When I heard someone on the radio talk about the orange glaze
on Fiestaware being, like the bomb, made from uranium and
dangerous, that's when I fell in love, and from time to time in
antique stores and junk shops I pick up a plate or two of that
color.

They're supposed to be slightly warm from the radioactivity,
but I haven't noticed. My mother knew little of what my father
did in those last years of the war, save that afterwards he disliked
anything radioactive—x-ray machines in shoe stores where you
could stare at the grey bones of your feet moving slowly on the
screen like slugs, and watches with glow-in-the-dark numbers—
both of which delighted my childhood until they too disappeared.

He died of cancer at the age I am now, though that had nothing
to do with his work, him being a theorist and all. My wife says
it seems too fitting, and people I tell nod knowingly about
that work and the bomb, which I think appalled my father. He
switched his field of study after the war. My mother can tell us
nothing of his reasons, but now I have these radioactive plates as
some slightly-warm memory of our family during the orange war,
proud of his work and of some history we could never mention
among ourselves in the way prisoners in the Japanese internment
camps never talk about what happened to them in those years.

Jan Severson in That Iowa Town

There were only six of us on the high school
tennis team for that smallish town
with its love for football and machinery.
I was sixth. I don't think
of you often; it's bad even to recall myself.
I never even found out how any of us
had come to learn tennis.

When something in a game went wrong
you threw your racquet hard
against the fence or into the woods
and the one time when our sometime coach
was in attendance he pleaded
like a child about to be punished
don't do it Jan don't don't

as the racquet sailed
on our wishes into the sky
perhaps where it still hangs.
We were shocked and secretly awed
you could get away with that.

The next day you'd do The Stroll
onto the court, racquet held like a guitar.
You drove a new '57 Chevy. I didn't
know many kids from your side of town or anyone
at all with a new car. I wonder
where it took you, wonder
at our own secret lives

I thought didn't matter, but
they say you are dying, and
when other people's children point one out
I can still tell the '55 from the '57, the car
seems part of my dreams,
incomplete as they are, the way the past
lingers in front of a house,
then, who knows, revs its engine
once, twice, and peels off down the street.

After More Than a Month

of despair, when a cigarette
seemed all could save me,
that month ago when I turned seventy
and the great god of lyric broke
poems in his soup, like crackers,
I wanted to write a love poem
to life itself. It's still never easy,
even after years sitting in the sunlight,
the delicacy of the feathery asparagus fronds

or the bad thoughts like criminals
after dark on the streets,
and the tricks the old masters
knew so well they practically fell out onto the page
like tiny silver fish rising in a dream
or small brown dogs, were all gone.
I am dying, Egypt, dying. Saudi Arabia, too,
if only I could remember where that was.
'In his soup' said a voice, 'like crackers.'

If I Could Tell You
I Would Let You Know

1

I wanted to be a charm-maker, a magician, wanted
to make spells and such, much more than just
poetry. Things that had true power.
protection. What a child I was;
poetry makes nothing happen, and yet. . . .

2

My grandmother and her son, my father,
both died of colon cancer. It's hardly amazing.
Given that heredity, I kept track,
and as a discipline endured visits
to doctors' offices and hospitals and

drank gallons of vile stuff. That should
have been enough. So it came
as a surprise to hear a woman
whose brother I knew fifty years back
mention her chemo. With the amount
of my concern, keeping up

with the latest scrap of cancer research,
everyone I know should have been
protected from that by my words.

3

There was a friend, trying to swim
in the Wisconsin River who drowned,

and animals I couldn't save.
That was different. I remembered,
thinking about the woman,

that she had freckles and was two years older.
It was said that after I lost my baby teeth
I should marry her, some childhood contract
I blushed at. Yet this one woman
comes to mind over and over these past weeks.

Time has failed her too. I am not sorry.
I wanted them all alive long enough
that I could grow to love them.
I thought. That's all I can say.

Joining the Circus

At the curb two large cottonwoods, a tree I've never
noticed since, named for the bits of fluff floating round
them. Ricky Johnson was my best friend

that summer, and I was invited for supper
at his house across the street,
with the trees, its rickety garage, and peeling white paint.

In the dark interior his father, a dark man,
and mother, smoked cigarettes, or that's what made it
seem dark, as in a painting. Stan

ran the sporting goods store, where I had watched
a game of the World Series on the TV there.
At dinner we have bread with our food, white

bread and soft butter, half a loaf on a plate for
anyone to take. At home, so distant,
we serve only the bread my mother's baked,

hard-crusted, never just piled in a stack,
and this soft, luscious, white bread is my first time
renouncing the bright dining room of home forever.

The Last One

The lawns and woods were still
in their winter shades of brown and gray.
While I was at the movie on Friday
it began to snow. Three inches of grainy stuff
covering the ground. Saint Patrick's Day. Around here,
that's the traditional time to plant peas.

By Sunday the top of the snow had melted or
blown away, exposing the first daffodils
blooming, their stalks scabbed and oozing,
the blossoms already wilted, but there they were.

Tuesday my brother-in-law called
to tell us that, after forty years,
my sister is divorcing him to marry
her college sweetheart.

It was a stroke
of lightning, changing everything.
As the weeks went on, the snow melted,
though small patches lingered,
near porches and heaps in parking lots
like something left from a movie with aliens.

I still need to finish these Christmas thank-you notes
my mother insisted on, even six years dead.
Not just a thank-you over the phone,
but real notes, before all the couples in my family split up,
before there is no way to write them.

At the Theater

As I walked into the unisex bathroom,
a young woman, leaving, held a stall door
open for me. I wanted brandy and cigars
ordered for everyone in the place.
From the others here, you could hear
the usual small exhalations and groans
—but an octave higher than I'm used to—
a true equality, an entire chorus
each with his or her fears

alone in the stalls like horses. Onstage,
the actor playing the Actor/Prince
and his friend were shuffling their way
through Croatia's second-most-popular
playwright at the turn of the century
and in a new translation.

As I walked out, a lovely woman
adjusting her make-up at a mirror asked
over her shoulder, "Where shall we go
afterwards?" My wife hates it
when I even dream like this.
She was so young, so lovely. I froze,
wondering why all my desires are caught up with fears
of losing whoever I have been for so long
that no amount of drama will change it,

and why in this place
she was asking me to walk out with her;
but the reply I couldn't quite catch
came from a woman somewhere behind me.

The Prince had still not found his old love,
though after the first act,
four percent of the spectators had left.
By intermission, over half of the audience,
drawn by this small fragment, this human drama,
was packed outside the bathroom.

Lullaby

A muffled cheering perhaps a mile off.
Just the crowd sounds, the dry leaves,
and the air almost dusty. Someone pacing
the yard. It was you. Lonely.

September, November, what is that nursery rhyme
you never thought you'd forget,
so never wrote it down? An odd thing
not to remember now, days, years.

The air carries that smell of childhood,
leaves burning. You have not smelled
that for a long time, and recognize it instantly.
Passing, passing.

From the high school now, half a mile away
come muted rhythmic sounds,
cheerleaders, or a marching band.
Old snowfall, heart fall.

You are not a part of them.
You are not part of the dry leaves.
One eye, then the other.
Lovely river, us together.

Humming

For those who stand in fortune's rays,
Every day's a holiday,
But the poor have only Christmas.

       —British music-hall song

I still hate the crumby orchestral
arrangements in Christmas concerts.
Sometimes they only happen every other year.
It's still too often. Always chimes,
and sleighbells. This year we didn't have
to rent a vibraphone, but something
called for claves, eight notes
I missed in the rush. What's tricky
is that the music's really drippy
and hard at the same time, all that
switching instruments, difficult not to get lost.

I like watching P. warm up the children's chorus
without them actually singing. It's really young kids,
about seven to nine years old—mostly girls.
In first-year Latin class we learned some carols
in the original Latin for a change.
I was a soprano until the tenth grade,
and tried to stay with the sopranos
until I couldn't hit the high notes anymore.

Years later, caroling with the other grown children
on our street, I could sort of still do
the men's harmonies but it was a strain.

I couldn't hear the parts right. "Adeste Fideles"
is the only Latin version I can remember now,
and precious little of that, from deep
in some closet along with the yearbooks.

Last week, driving home, the radio had this perfectly
simple version of some carol, just the original
vocal harmonies, no claves, no smushy violins.
Without thinking, I found myself
in a cracked, off-key voice I hadn't used
for a long time, humming along.

Falling in Love

One of the delights our planet offers
to older and younger,
both the same. The young do not think so,

all curves and curls. But here they are, this couple
my age, touching hands with the same flush
of color and wonder as where I married my love.

Someone wanders the house alone or sits,
and everything suddenly becomes
joyous as sleep or the darkness promised

in evenings or late afternoons by sunlight.
You wake early, say. It is dark outside. By the light
of the stove, you make coffee and get ready

for a walk. It has snowed or it is
going to snow. The lawns and winter trees
are darks and white. Then, slowly, a hint

of color, a distant stoplight turns green: Gradually
one more time, the world becomes beautiful.
This is how love works, how each day

there are chances for the usual miracles:
the daylilies in the grass, the red geraniums:
touch and colors and the words of our vows

exactly as we practiced in school, the small voices
these two conjugate once more for each other.
He sings. She sings. They do. Sing love.

Letter to Howard Levy

Last weekend I was helping
at a local art opening (good food, nasty wine)
when I noticed a girl quietly reading
off to one side, oblivious to the people milling around.
Nothing so remarkable about her, pretty,
in a blue dress, still young enough
you couldn't tell what she'd look like as an adult.

I moved close enough
to see the book, an older one
judging from what I caught of the typeface
and yellowing paper, *Mozart*.
She looked up from what it said only
at the flash from a photographer
who'd spotted her the same time I had,
and went on reading. That girl, alone,
her summer dress and her concentration, reminded me
that you healed yourself once
of some heartbreak I never heard the details of,

that you did it listening to Mozart
over and over. I think that his music
finally must have filled you so completely
there was no room anymore for your particular pain.

I always hope that people I love
will be made beautiful by that love, or happy.
That I will be happy. That it will help.
And I admire that sense you have
of what might lead us to take up our rightful lives

like a crutch thrown down in disgust,
not so much healed as able to get around
in our bodies again.

Mostly the rest of us go on playing and re-playing
the same small songs we thought would help, but there's
hardly any real music in hours of that.
No wonder we're never restored in any way
that might last more than the few minutes
a song takes. Half the time I don't even know
what made me want to hear something,
even my own ragged heart.

Winter Nights, the
Stars Pinched and Cold

That afternoon four brown pelicans
followed each other, wings rigid
and unmoving, as each rose and fell
on the thermals crossing the landscape,
huge, elegant gliders strung into one waving line,
passing forever. Goodbye, goodbye.

"Nothing for you today," said the Muse,
dropping a handful of bills and third-class offers
not to be passed up on the hallway table,
and smiled. She's taken to doing that
since the medication started. I feel nothing.

Lately, I've been thinking about passion;
not about it, exactly, but how some people
toss away a great life for a new love,
an exciting affair or the torment of adventure,
as if they cannot stop themselves.

The dog's learned
to open the refrigerator by himself.
He seems penitent afterwards, that's all.
I only write, it seems, when the Muse is not here.
Sounds grim, you say? You ain't seen nothing.

The World from the
Silcox Hut, Mount Hood

On top of a stone, a pebble really,
is a small white cap like a cloud.
The clouds outside the window
are beginning to rise
and float along the mountainside,
and in the distance
bumps of white poke out
from the gray of the sky.

But we have not come to
the point yet. This stone
longs to be a volcano rising over dark land,
older and already cold.
The volcano will say nothing
but go on breathing in
and out, slowly, so as not
to be heard. Volcanoes
do not like being overheard,
though the clouds do not care
who hears their days. Cloud stories are large.

They forget, however,
that they themselves will fade,
dissolve in an instant.
The mountain, this rock
is not like that. Not at all.
It will stay awake all
this night, watching, listening
for something. I am its only friend.

Taking on the Past

It is late at night and the sky
a black space seen from the desk,
cloudy. The telephone rings, the future
wants to say hello;
something about the past.
It's been warned
not to do this anymore, asked time
and tune again. The police
are no help, your friends have told you
they would not be. Let it ring.

The stars recently seem smaller,
less bright than in summer.
It's just an illusion, or the way the mind
operates when frightened. Still,
you have to love the way the past gets honored,
the women and men I loved or let down or who moved away,
though now they are all over sixty. Shh, they are
asleep. Odd they don't look
a day over whenever you last saw them.

It is safe in the past, the footprints
you stepped in still visible.
You could take a walk in the dark,
take the dog who, when the wind is right,
can foretell the future. Or walk
by yourself. Oh, go ahead, see what the phone wants.

Elegy in March

I have spent fifty years wondering
whether anything is beautiful because we say so.
At the end of winter, the grass
was turning almost "pre-spring," muddy,
gray-brown, the way, oddly, pre-writing
is done by children using a pencil,
and pre-drilling holes requires a drill,
some little bit of spirit
involved in the brown camouflage
covering the lawns and fields, to be thrown off
like jungle netting hiding an airfield
and its planes somewhere in the Pacific,
the enemy bombers gone.

Odd, all these things—that almost overnight the
red-winged blackbirds are back
in the fields—to mention in a letter.
Not that I wrote her often,
but I'd look around for something like that,
as if the earth were our dish of ice cream
to share, and the birds and flowers
memories from somewhere we'd been
when I was a child.

Driving us in the mountains, me half certain
we'd wander off the road and fall,
it was beautiful, my mother said. Making
that up, I thought, dry
and sandy and way below,
maybe a dry stream bed.

I wish it were not my face in the mirror,
I do not like it. Not quite me, I think
every time I see it staring back,
though the obvious would be to ask who it is
that I want to look like. My mother gave me this face,
no one I could say I know.

Stories

Fail not, at your Peril, it began,
the subpoena a friend got, years back.
Really. No less than *peril*.
I don't know how that phrase came to mind,
the thin, satin strap of an evening gown
slipping its way down a lovely shoulder.

Not that my friends get a lot
of subpoenas, though that
might make me seem intriguing.
No, this one was to testify
about how long a freight train
had been blocking some street near
where he lived. Someone

had complained, and there was a law
about how long this train could block the road.
He loved the language of the thing,
and I love the way you can back yourself

into a story or out of it
by the silky tracks of these puzzles in syntax.
I mean, it was Einstein who said
that to truly explain one thing, you'd have
to explain everything in the universe.

And we're not even down to
why a word like peril, whatever it really
means, has survived so long.
Fail, now that brings up something different.

Melancholy

"We've come," the woman calls out, "to listen
silently to the river." Drawings
of flowers and fish made by children
hang from branches beyond the mowed strip
where thin trees have grown up, hiding the water.

The sound of cars murmurs along the highway
laid out in front of these grand,
ruined houses leading toward the Capital.
There is no other sound, no river,
only whatever we carry in our hearts called *river*.

A friend returns to say she's found
small animal tracks along the bank.
I do not go see the tracks
though as we say (but do not, since we've been asked
to be silent), this woman's heart
is in the right place. As we pass by,

a rush of sparrows sweeps into the branches.
Without prompting, I can accept
only what my guarded nature allows me.
The day swelters, filled with jewelweed
and spicebush edging toward the water.
I wish it were otherwise, the highway,
its houses, the heart silent as a river.

My Blue Heaven

(William Matthews, 1942–1997)

"Ah, all the elves are at the toyshop," he said,
looking up as he approached the porch,
meaning, I thought then, to refer to the others
as mischief-makers, revelers, fellow weirdoes,
which of course they were, and he was too,
and flashed us a look of expensive laughter
so eloquent only a clown or child could've done it.

Like money, he kept us in circulation.
His lines dazzled and we clapped our hands
with delight, full of envy and joy
at what he could do. So much we didn't know
how to say, or to avoid saying,
he put into words for us like an amused parent
helping the kids with an assignment.

Each poem seemed both new and familiar
as the girl of our dreams, who is, he remarked
once, the worst possible woman to marry,
and we did anyway, and didn't he
know it, didn't he ramble, didn't he?
What could you expect from someone who dealt
in "stand-up tragedy," as he thought of the art?

With him seemed to go whole jazz recordings.
Nights of music he liked to think of
himself as part of, playing chorus

after chorus on one number or another,
suddenly ceased to exist, vanished,
as if he'd only conjured them up, while we
thumb through his books, hoping to find traces of them.

Now we patrons at the Bar of the Flattened
Heart, each of us left fumbling over old songs,
turning over memories like small change,
we will have to learn to get on without him.
And why not? We have each other, of course,
and our own self, that constant
companion to be true to, if we cared to
or could remember how. Why not? All the elves
are at the toyshop. All but the one.

Silences

1

When the man arrived at the door of the house
where he'd come for dinner, the hostess kissed him.
He wondered if she really wanted to kiss him; it could have
been just habit, that perfunctory kiss grownups practiced,
nothing more than hello. Did that
make him blush, or was it something else? Later
in the evening, he doubted he'd ever know.

2

The concert was called "operatic favorites," which
meant that the percussionists hated the music—not
because they disliked it or were unfamiliar
but because it was so hard to keep counting rests
without being distracted. If one knew
to watch for it, you could see the players
counting with each other during the music,
that fear of being wrong. It showed
in a certain determination, worried,
they would say, that someone would hear a mistake.

3

While I was talking with my friend, he walked over
and came up behind her. She must have met him before,
because she said hello. Perhaps she was brought up
that way and was trying to be polite. He handed her
a postcard with a poem on the back. She thanked him.

After a second's hesitation, he handed me
a copy. It was right around the election, and I glanced
at the flag on the back, thinking, Oh, not another,
but he moved off. And I was grateful.

November 1

Like a squirrel, one brown
leaf wandered into the street
and a black car ran over it,
then another one drifted out.
Driving along that afternoon,
I saw a monarch butterfly overhead,
probably heading for the Yucatan:
that heavy straight-ahead flutter
you might think of as a flighty
concentration, or as a kind of freedom

—the way I look at some bad thing,
something stupid from long ago, a lie,
say, or some woman I failed—
and the embarrassment keeps you
from despair, the shame
you know your mind won't
let you dwell on long. It keeps you moving.
On the tree beside an apartment building
the leaves are thin, discolored.
The grass needs a wash, too.

The hot-dog vendors all push their carts
at the same time along the side-streets
toward some destination on the West Side.
The light is heavy over the small gingkoes
and sycamores someone from the City
must have planted among so much
pavement, and the butterfly glowing
over it all. Darkness will return.

Making Up a New Bed

I went back to pick up the last
of the books shoved in a closet.
Emptied of old clothes and arguments
the place seemed different.
I avoided passing the bedroom
with its thousands of stories,
an entire *Arabian Nights*
I could not bear someone else hearing.

By the telephone I found a note
she'd left herself on an envelope:
Only a rat would run out on you
when you need him.
It wasn't how I'd tell the story.
Now, clumsily, I will begin to take back my
name, and she hers, not quite sure
whom they mean. No one will telephone,
and begin with "it's me."

At the end of the evening,
we are, each of us, the heroes
of our own adventures,
revising the stories to make a happy ending.
With material this thin, who
but a rat would take on such work?

The State Capital

Now I think about it one of the loveliest
women I ever met grew up in Des Moines,
so there must be things I don't know about the place.
We ate at Bishops' Cafeteria somewhere in Des Moines;
my father never minded the food, for me always
mashed potatoes and chocolate milk, though my mother

did not care for lunch and was there to buy clothes.
It took us over an hour to get to Des Moines,
the nearest city to us, in our new car a color
my mother called chartreuse, and I had to practice that.
Did other Iowans pronounce it with an "s" as Des Moines?
Even before crossing over the muddy Des Moines

River you drove through block after block, everything that
same color, and gradually into downtown.
First we passed the Lawsonomy Institute of Des Moines
at which my mother mentioned some kind of medicine
(chiropractic? herbalism?) we must never think of trying.
Many people must've been misled.

On the way to Younkers Department Store, or was it
spelled Yonkers as in New York, we walked by the *Des Moines
Register* building; that was the paper we took though I
delivered the *Ames Daily Tribune* and only Sundays the *Register*.
Somehow my parents learned that Younkers
had enormous glazed doughnuts for later on. In Des Moines

I bought some clothes for school, probably from the same
salesman who later got my mother to buy this narrow

one-inch black necktie she sent me that was "all the rage
back east" where I was the only boy with one. For children
there were escalators to ride on in Des Moines
so escalators have never been difficult.

As we grew older we would often drive across Des Moines
to where the lawns became green again and to the Art
Museum. Once they had a nude by Goya in Des Moines, I wonder
if she saw it too behind the special curtain.

A Calder-like mobile is what I remember of that Des Moines.
Years later I saw one hanging in an office
in New York. Certain no one actually owned one,
I asked who had made it and was told only "Calder."
I do not think I shall find that woman again.

The Penis and Me

Memory is not a consolation for experience
but a philosophical problem.

—Stanley Plumly

Trying to recall one lovely body
or another, what comes to remind me
is rarely more than the frantic grasp,

that fierce and tender light, when what I'm seeking
is more like the curve of a shoulder or breast, skin's
brightness. I missed out, my mind tells me,

or at least I did in those days. Now,
when I want to become a sculptor, a worshiper
of the body's architecture, all that

is unavailable. The penis
is a dull biographer, Bill Matthews said;
what it knows of sex is merely arithmetic.

And nothing's left but the barest outlines—
names, perhaps years with their corners
worn and scratched like old furniture.

I am trying to remember how life felt,
and this comes back to the lightness of skin
on someone I don't even know, that's all.

I must be trying to preserve the world, feelings and shadow,
and find something else in that,
and the moments in one bed or another,

even a snowy field in March, seconds
of thrill and feverish movement. I want
to create a body, one that includes me.
I still can't recall what position
I woke up in this morning, and by the time
I am awake and standing, it is gone
beyond knowing how I lay down last night.

A Bottle of Wine,
New Year's Day

The other rooms and the kitchen stuff
had been dismantled and rearranged
by friends who'd come and cleared out
the house, that museum of our cluttered lives,
to make it beautiful. They'd even taken
the pots and pans from over the counter
and put in their place the large mixer
we only use twice a year, for God's sake.
The pans were now
scattered around the stove.
They hung our pictures in new places
and rearranged the mantle and its sculptures.

I asked my wife if she wanted our pots
to stay that way; she said, yes, she did,
so I went on to something else, shaking
my head at this waste, this folly.

This morning I understood
this difficult arrangement
she wanted left
as a tribute to that dozen friends,
their long day of heavy work
hauling bag after bag to the trash.
What joy they'd taken
in helping us to a new life,
to see how love walks into a house
and removes everything dead.

About Rabbits

Rabbits do not appear in dreams, at least not anyone's I know of.

Flopsy, Mopsy, someone, and Peter.
Most people nowadays have never seen a rabbit.
Often their sensitive eyes are used to test drugs.

Rabbits have babies every six weeks;
there is an expression, to multiply like rabbits.
They scream awfully, I gather, when threatened or hurt.

My sister's family kept one, and I was surprised
by how much personality he had, if not trainable.
His eyes were red, but that didn't seem frightening.

I read that someone long ago injected
dyes into the veins in rabbits' ears, seeking
medical cures. I hope it didn't kill the rabbits.

Rabbits were introduced to Australia to get rid
of something and instead became a plague themselves
though my mother, who lived there, never mentions them.

The term "introduce" sounds funny,
as if rabbits were brought to meet someone;
also "multiply," which seems too much for rabbits.

Rabbits suffer from myxomatosis—
what a lovely name for a disease.
Or is that what ended their introduction?

My father never said much about his life.
One of his colleagues said he didn't realize
the enormity of what they'd done until the evening

after that first atomic bomb test. He'd had to drive
into the desert. Coming back, in the headlights he counted
eighty-four rabbits flattened in the road.

My father tested me on a lot of things
though I know more about rabbits than about him.

We had rabbit for dinner once. I don't know
why my mother, who was a great cook, served it.
I couldn't eat any. I have not tried it since.

Overture

I saw the pictures of Iowa under water.
Our whole family drove to Des Moines once
to see *West Side Story* at the movie theater,
and afterwards, as we stood in the bleached daylight,
my youngest sister asked if we could
snap our fingers as the dancers had.
I do not know if she wanted us to snarl,
"We're Jets!" at the same time,
but we laughed at her; we knew
we were Jets, and that the street was ours.

The grubby city has probably vanished
under the recent floodwaters, gone;
the theater, too, dead and dark as mud,
and you will probably not even remember
that evening along the pavement,
me suddenly all grown up, our other sister,
and our father and mother smiling at each other,
pleased in the warm daylight, our family
for once not fighting or sullen, that they had survived
all the grimy sidewalks and the winters
of an Iowa life they had somehow been thrown into.

I thought of this last night
at my final orchestra performance for the year,
which opened with a selection from *West Side Story*
—though not the wild and lovely overture—
and there they were, the songs that made me weep,
though I've never figured out why their power
has lasted so long, as if I could not, even now,
stand anything that might be lost, anything beautiful, that is.

Straight No Chaser

It is interesting to note that in early writings
mentioning jazz, people are often appalled
by the loudness of the drums.

The story ends, so far as it has an ending,
in an orchestral rehearsal with someone
handing out parts to *My Fair Lady* and *Oklahoma*,
those songs from the musicals, long
lost love celebrating itself with the musicians.
It has been so long since she thought of them,
she's surprised these shows still exist, or ever did.

She recalls her parents' friends
standing around their piano. Sometimes
they are singing verses about academic life
set to Gilbert & Sullivan tunes, or choruses from *South Pacific*.
Where did they hear about the torments of love?
She could not understand why anyone
felt sad, or glorious, listening to Grieg or Schumann.

In 1955, "On the Street Where You Live"
from *My Fair Lady* was a Top Forties hit
sung by Vic Damone; she still knew the words,
so it must have been important. But she had really liked
the clash of hearts in the new rock and roll.
It was savage, she could feel the struggle
without knowing why. Your body set to music.

Think of the excitement of *Damn Yankees*, only
beloved because you could look into the pit

and see how the drummer used his sticks
on the railing for the sounds in "I've Got
(clank clank clank clank) Steam Heat."

And how that boy had invited her to sit
with him in the orchestra pit for
The Pirates of Penzance, and she had heard
for the first time "Ah, Leave Me Not to Pine."
The sadness must have been there long
before loss itself showed up.

She must have known, even before
it happened, that he would leave her
for someone else he'd fallen for,
and she had only the words left over
to feel her way. Just this.

And here we are at the beginning.
Each of our stories, our lives,
we would say, starts like a voyage.
You stand by the ship's railing looking out,
wondering where the disappointment of love
shows up for the first time. In songs, of course.

"There Is Augury in the
Fall of a Sparrow"

Fifty years after that last lot had been packed off
to the new world and good riddance to them,
someone in London decided, in a fit
of generosity the English are known for,
to send something familiar with them, like a picture,
or a few tiny flower seeds a mother

might tuck into some corner of a suitcase,
to remind them of what they'd left. Birds,
English birds they might have seen
on their way to the fields or factories.
That was it! The familiar birds they knew,
even just to eat if nothing else was around.

So the Society for Acclimatization
to America formed a complete list
of all birds mentioned in Shakespeare.
Perhaps the refugees had even heard
scraps of him in whatever schools
might have briefly held them.

Why not, say, from Wordsworth? Or even
the government, this list? Were the birds dying out
in the thin forests of those English villages
the immigrants had come here from,
where the trees had long since gone
for ship masts and beams and factories?

It is enough, perhaps, that the Society
determined to make a modern Ark,

two of each kind of bird from the list, sent over here.
Surely the workers would rejoice
at these creatures from home, even the starlings,
the clouds of their mottled coats and stubby wings.

Surely, they must've thought there'd be some
corner of New Jersey near our home town,
that was forever England; until last week
someone had the starlings poisoned
as a threat to the farmers, as well as
to the cowardly but pretty bluebirds. Surely,
someone slightly misguided loves us all.

Gift Wrap

So silent out. Even the stars
have stopped giving heat, leaving only
their pale dots of light in the mysterious quiet.
This is not anything new, just
another early morning, the streets
silent with snow and the small steam of breathing.
The absence of birds in the distance,
that, too, seems personal, the world's neighbors
hiding behind their curtains, numb fingers.
You can even hear the sound
your hands make as you slip them
into your coat pockets.

Wrapping a package, I suddenly
remembered the young woman teaching me
how to do that neatly, an art in itself. She lived
up the street from my family and
watching her wrap a book or some other gift
was as if she had been born
with some sense of decoration, of beauty
I could only imitate. Think of all
the years I have had a crush on her,
or that's the way it seems. The dance
of learning, you might call it. By now
it's an automatic fumble, wrapping paper
all over the table, and tape, and ribbon.

Nothing speaks to us now; the world's become
a child determined to let out
not one word, withdrawn, face flushed
and victorious. Memory or the future

seem only silly directions. The divorced man
down the street thinks he wants a new life,
but he pictures it as his old life, exactly—
coffee in that little place before work,
a walk in the autumn sunshine—
in some way that seems suddenly
happier to him. I wished him a Merry Christmas.
What the hell do I know?

Acknowledgments

I am grateful to the editors of the journals in which versions of the following poems first appeared:

Barrow Street: "About the State Capital," "Jan Severson in That Iowa Town," "My Blue Heaven"

Edison Review: "An Anniversarie," "The Last One," "'There Is Augury in the Fall of a Sparrow'"

Graven Images: "Melancholy"

Iowa Review: "About Rabbits"

Schuylkill Valley Journal of the Arts: "Joining the Circus

Sou'wester: "Elegy in March," "Taking On the Past"

U.S. 1 Worksheets: "At the Theater," "As the Twelfth Armored Division Enters the Capital," "The Octopus," "The World from the Silcox Hut, Mount Hood"

"Letter to Howard Levy" appeared in *The Breath of Parted Lips: Voices from the Robert Frost Place*, vol. 2, ed. Sydney Lea (CavanKerry Press, 2004). "Melancholy" appeared in *Urban Nature: Poems about Wildlife in the City*, ed. Laure-Anne Bosselaar (Milkweed Editions, 2000). "My Blue Heaven" appeared in *Blues for Bill: A Tribute to the Memory of William Matthews*, ed. Kurt Brown, Meg Kearney, and

Donna Reis (University of Akron Press, 2005). "Joining the Circus" appeared in *Never Before: Poems about First Experiences*, ed. Laure-Anne Bossclaar (Four Way Books, 2005).

I am also grateful to the Virginia Center for the Creative Arts, which offered me a residency, and to the Lawrenceville Poetry Group. Special thanks are due to Jim Reigel, Richard Tayson, and Baron Wormser.

CavanKerry's Mission

CavanKerry Press is a not-for-profit literary press dedicated to art and community. From its inception in 2000, its vision has been to present, through poetry and prose, *Lives Brought to Life* and to create programs that bring CavanKerry books and writers to diverse audiences.

Other Books in the Notable Voices Series

Printing this book on 30-percent PCW and FSC certified paper saved 2 trees, 1 million BTUs of energy, 127 pounds of CO_2, 67 pounds of solid waste, and 524 gallons of water.